Daily Inspiration

A Good Heart Journal

To

The Greatest Kid On The Planet

"If you can see it, you can be it."

Dear Gentle Spirit,

I am so happy you've chosen the Daily Inspiration Journal from The Good Heart. Creating this journal brought me so much joy, and I hope it will be a source of encouragement and inspiration for you.

For me, this journal serves as a gentle reminder to express gratitude for all of the wonderful things I am surrounded by each day. I know gratitude is the most powerful force I have at my disposal, and when I express appreciation in earnest, the Universe responds and allows even more wonderful and amazing things to enter into my life.

Over the years, I've learned the answer to every question we ask the Universe is "yes". We all have the ability to live our very best life and to achieve our heart's desires. The key to our happiness lies within us, within our hearts, within our thoughts, and within our intentions. Our thoughts are our own, and it is up to us to choose how we use them. We are powerful beings, and we have the divine energy of the Universe at our fingertips. When we choose love and gratitude, and healing and understanding, when we choose to look forward into our future with hope and anticipation for all that is ahead of us, and when we trust that all we wish for is on its way, we become deliberate creators, and we can create a life that is everything we could hope for.

This is the reason I created this journal, to remind us that our thoughts create our life, and when we choose positive thoughts, wonderful things happen. And so we can rest assured in the certainty that, at every moment, we are loved and supported, and we are worthy and deserving and capable of creating everything we desire.

The Universe is waiting eagerly to respond to each and every one of us, to our thoughts and our feelings, and to our dreams and intentions. It wants to bring us everything we wish for. So, when you write in this journal, I hope you fill it with love. And I hope you fill it with joy. I hope you fill it with your dreams and your passions, and with your hopes for the future. And when you do, I hope you know all of those things are on their way to you. I know amazing things are going to happen for you.

I am sincerely yours,

M.C. Greene

I have the power to choose

my thoughts and create

the life I desire.

Date: ___ / ___ / _____

Gratitude brings wonderful things into my life.

Today, I am grateful for:

_____
_____
_____
_____

I have the power to choose my thoughts and create my life.

Today, I will focus on:

_____
_____
_____
_____
_____

The Universe is on my side and is always working on my behalf.

I know the Universe is helping me to:

_____
_____
_____
_____

If I can see it and believe in it, I know I can achieve it.

I am in the process of:

_____

_____

_____

_____

_____

_____

I will end each day with positive thoughts and excitement for all that is to come.

Something that made me happy today was:

_____

_____

_____

_____

_____

I am loved. I am valued. I am worthy.

I know I am:

_____

_____

_____

_____

Date: ___ / ___ / ____

I am so thankful for the way my life is unfolding.

Today, I am grateful for:

_____

_____

_____

_____

I know my thoughts become my life.

Today, I will focus on:

_____

_____

_____

_____

_____

The Universe loves me and wants to bring me all I desire.

I know the Universe is helping me to:

_____

_____

_____

_____

_____

There is nothing I cannot do, have, or be.

I am in the process of:

_____

_____

_____

_____

_____

_____

Each new day is an opportunity to make something wonderful happen.

Something that made me happy today was:

_____

_____

_____

_____

_____

I am surrounded by people who love me and choose me.

I know I am:

_____

_____

_____

_____

Date: ___ /___ /____

I welcome peace, love, and joy into my life.

Today, I am grateful for:

_____

_____

_____

_____

I know positive thoughts turn into positive outcomes.

Today, I will focus on:

_____

_____

_____

_____

_____

I trust the process. Everything comes to me in perfect timing.

I know the Universe is helping me to:

_____

_____

_____

_____

_____

I know success is inevitable. New doors open for me every day.

I am in the process of:

_____

_____

_____

_____

_____

_____

I am grateful for where I am and excited for where I am going.

Something that made me happy today was:

_____

_____

_____

_____

_____

I am everything I need to be. Always.

I know I am:

_____

_____

_____

_____

Date: ___ /___ /_____

I am at peace and in harmony with all I am and all I have.

Today, I am grateful for:

_____

_____

_____

_____

I let go of doubt and fear and celebrate all that is going my way.

Today, I will focus on:

_____

_____

_____

_____

_____

I am loved and worthy of having all I desire.

I know the Universe is helping me to:

_____

_____

_____

_____

_____

I know there are no limits to all I can be and achieve.

I am in the process of:

_____

_____

_____

_____

_____

_____

*Today was a wonderful day. Tomorrow
will be even better.*

Something that made me happy today was:

_____

_____

_____

_____

_____

I am capable. I am strong. I am powerful. I am brave.

I know I am:

_____

_____

_____

_____

Date: ___ / ___ / ____

Gratitude brings wonderful things into my life.

Today, I am grateful for:

_____

_____

_____

_____

I have the power to choose my thoughts and create my life.

Today, I will focus on:

_____

_____

_____

_____

_____

The Universe is on my side and is always working on my behalf.

I know the Universe is helping me to:

_____

_____

_____

_____

_____

If I can see it and believe in it, I know I can achieve it.

I am in the process of:

_____

_____

_____

_____

_____

_____

I will end each day with positive thoughts and excitement for all that is to come.

Something that made me happy today was:

_____

_____

_____

_____

I am loved. I am valued. I am worthy.

I know I am:

_____

_____

_____

_____

Date: ___ /___ /____

I am so thankful for the way my life is unfolding.

Today, I am grateful for:

_____

_____

_____

_____

I know my thoughts become my life.

Today, I will focus on:

_____

_____

_____

_____

_____

The Universe loves me and wants to bring me all I desire.

I know the Universe is helping me to:

_____

_____

_____

_____

_____

There is nothing I cannot do, have, or be.

I am in the process of:

_____

_____

_____

_____

_____

_____

Each new day is an opportunity to make something wonderful happen.

Something that made me happy today was:

_____

_____

_____

_____

_____

I am surrounded by people who love me and choose me.

I know I am:

_____

_____

_____

_____

Date: ___ /___ /____

I welcome peace, love, and joy into my life.

Today, I am grateful for:

_____

_____

_____

_____

I know positive thoughts turn into positive outcomes.

Today, I will focus on:

_____

_____

_____

_____

_____

I trust the process. Everything comes to me in perfect timing.

I know the Universe is helping me to:

_____

_____

_____

_____

_____

I know success is inevitable. New doors open for me every day.

I am in the process of:

_____

_____

_____

_____

_____

_____

I am grateful for where I am and excited for where I am going.

Something that made me happy today was:

_____

_____

_____

_____

I am everything I need to be. Always.

I know I am:

_____

_____

_____

_____

Date: ___ / ___ / ____

I am at peace and in harmony with all I am and all I have.

Today, I am grateful for:

_____

_____

_____

_____

I let go of doubt and fear and celebrate all that is going my way.

Today, I will focus on:

_____

_____

_____

_____

_____

I am loved and worthy of having all I desire.

I know the Universe is helping me to:

_____

_____

_____

_____

_____

I know there are no limits to all I can be and achieve.

I am in the process of:

_____

_____

_____

_____

_____

_____

*Today was a wonderful day. Tomorrow
will be even better.*

Something that made me happy today was:

_____

_____

_____

_____

_____

I am capable. I am strong. I am powerful. I am brave.

I know I am:

_____

_____

_____

_____

Date: ___ /___ /____

Gratitude brings wonderful things into my life.

Today, I am grateful for:

_____

_____

_____

_____

I have the power to choose my thoughts and create my life.

Today, I will focus on:

_____

_____

_____

_____

_____

The Universe is on my side and is always working on my behalf.

I know the Universe is helping me to:

_____

_____

_____

_____

_____

If I can see it and believe in it, I know I can achieve it.

I am in the process of:

_____

_____

_____

_____

_____

_____

I will end each day with positive thoughts and excitement for all that is to come.

Something that made me happy today was:

_____

_____

_____

_____

I am loved. I am valued. I am worthy.

I know I am:

_____

_____

_____

_____

Date: ___ /___ /____

I am so thankful for the way my life is unfolding.

Today, I am grateful for:

_____

_____

_____

_____

I know my thoughts become my life.

Today, I will focus on:

_____

_____

_____

_____

_____

_____

The Universe loves me and wants to bring me all I desire.

I know the Universe is helping me to:

_____

_____

_____

_____

_____

_____

There is nothing I cannot do, have, or be.

I am in the process of:

_____

_____

_____

_____

_____

_____

Each new day is an opportunity to make something wonderful happen.

Something that made me happy today was:

_____

_____

_____

_____

_____

I am surrounded by people who love me and choose me.

I know I am:

_____

_____

_____

_____

Date: ___ / ___ / ____

I welcome peace, love, and joy into my life.

Today, I am grateful for:

_____

_____

_____

_____

I know positive thoughts turn into positive outcomes.

Today, I will focus on:

_____

_____

_____

_____

_____

I trust the process. Everything comes to me in perfect timing.

I know the Universe is helping me to:

_____

_____

_____

_____

_____

I know success is inevitable. New doors open for me every day.

I am in the process of:

_____

_____

_____

_____

_____

_____

I am grateful for where I am and excited for where I am going.

Something that made me happy today was:

_____

_____

_____

_____

_____

I am everything I need to be. Always.

I know I am:

_____

_____

_____

_____

Date: ___ /___ /____

I am at peace and in harmony with all I am and all I have.

Today, I am grateful for:

_____

_____

_____

_____

I let go of doubt and fear and celebrate all that is going my way.

Today, I will focus on:

_____

_____

_____

_____

_____

I am loved and worthy of having all I desire.

I know the Universe is helping me to:

_____

_____

_____

_____

_____

I know there are no limits to all I can be and achieve.

I am in the process of:

_____

_____

_____

_____

_____

_____

Today was a wonderful day. Tomorrow
will be even better.

Something that made me happy today was:

_____

_____

_____

_____

_____

I am capable. I am strong. I am powerful. I am brave.

I know I am:

_____

_____

_____

_____

Date: ___ / ___ / _____

Gratitude brings wonderful things into my life.

Today, I am grateful for:

_____

_____

_____

_____

I have the power to choose my thoughts and create my life.

Today, I will focus on:

_____

_____

_____

_____

_____

The Universe is on my side and is always working on my behalf.

I know the Universe is helping me to:

_____

_____

_____

_____

_____

If I can see it and believe in it, I know I can achieve it.

I am in the process of:

_____

_____

_____

_____

_____

_____

*I will end each day with positive thoughts and excitement for
all that is to come.*

Something that made me happy today was:

_____

_____

_____

_____

I am loved. I am valued. I am worthy.

I know I am:

_____

_____

_____

_____

Date: ___ /___ /____

I am so thankful for the way my life is unfolding.

Today, I am grateful for:

_____

_____

_____

_____

I know my thoughts become my life.

Today, I will focus on:

_____

_____

_____

_____

_____

The Universe loves me and wants to bring me all I desire.

I know the Universe is helping me to:

_____

_____

_____

_____

_____

There is nothing I cannot do, have, or be.

I am in the process of:

_____

_____

_____

_____

_____

_____

Each new day is an opportunity to make something wonderful happen.

Something that made me happy today was:

_____

_____

_____

_____

_____

I am surrounded by people who love me and choose me.

I know I am:

_____

_____

_____

_____

Date: ___ /___ /____

I welcome peace, love, and joy into my life.

Today, I am grateful for:

_____

_____

_____

_____

I know positive thoughts turn into positive outcomes.

Today, I will focus on:

_____

_____

_____

_____

_____

I trust the process. Everything comes to me in perfect timing.

I know the Universe is helping me to:

_____

_____

_____

_____

_____

I know success is inevitable. New doors open for me every day.

I am in the process of:

_____

_____

_____

_____

_____

_____

I am grateful for where I am and excited for where I am going.

Something that made me happy today was:

_____

_____

_____

_____

I am everything I need to be. Always.

I know I am:

_____

_____

_____

_____

Date: ___ /___ /____

I am at peace and in harmony with all I am and all I have.

Today, I am grateful for:

_____

_____

_____

_____

I let go of doubt and fear and celebrate all that is going my way.

Today, I will focus on:

_____

_____

_____

_____

_____

I am loved and worthy of having all I desire.

I know the Universe is helping me to:

_____

_____

_____

_____

_____

I know there are no limits to all I can be and achieve.

I am in the process of:

_____

_____

_____

_____

_____

_____

*Today was a wonderful day. Tomorrow
will be even better.*

Something that made me happy today was:

_____

_____

_____

_____

_____

I am capable. I am strong. I am powerful. I am brave.

I know I am:

_____

_____

_____

_____

Date: ___ /___ /____

Gratitude brings wonderful things into my life.

Today, I am grateful for:

_____

_____

_____

_____

I have the power to choose my thoughts and create my life.

Today, I will focus on:

_____

_____

_____

_____

_____

The Universe is on my side and is always working on my behalf.

I know the Universe is helping me to:

_____

_____

_____

_____

_____

If I can see it and believe in it, I know I can achieve it.

I am in the process of:

_____

_____

_____

_____

_____

_____

I will end each day with positive thoughts and excitement for all that is to come.

Something that made me happy today was:

_____

_____

_____

_____

I am loved. I am valued. I am worthy.

I know I am:

_____

_____

_____

_____

Date: ___ /___ /____

I am so thankful for the way my life is unfolding.

Today, I am grateful for:

_____

_____

_____

_____

I know my thoughts become my life.

Today, I will focus on:

_____

_____

_____

_____

_____

The Universe loves me and wants to bring me all I desire.

I know the Universe is helping me to:

_____

_____

_____

_____

_____

There is nothing I cannot do, have, or be.

I am in the process of:

_____

_____

_____

_____

_____

_____

Each new day is an opportunity to make something wonderful happen.

Something that made me happy today was:

_____

_____

_____

_____

_____

I am surrounded by people who love me and choose me.

I know I am:

_____

_____

_____

_____

Date: ___ / ___ / ____

I welcome peace, love, and joy into my life.

Today, I am grateful for:

_____

_____

_____

_____

I know positive thoughts turn into positive outcomes.

Today, I will focus on:

_____

_____

_____

_____

_____

I trust the process. Everything comes to me in perfect timing.

I know the Universe is helping me to:

_____

_____

_____

_____

_____

I know success is inevitable. New doors open for me every day.

I am in the process of:

_____

_____

_____

_____

_____

_____

I am grateful for where I am and excited for where I am going.

Something that made me happy today was:

_____

_____

_____

_____

_____

I am everything I need to be. Always.

I know I am:

_____

_____

_____

_____

Date: ___ /___ /____

I am at peace and in harmony with all I am and all I have.

Today, I am grateful for:

_____

_____

_____

_____

I let go of doubt and fear and celebrate all that is going my way.

Today, I will focus on:

_____

_____

_____

_____

_____

I am loved and worthy of having all I desire.

I know the Universe is helping me to:

_____

_____

_____

_____

_____

I know there are no limits to all I can be and achieve.

I am in the process of:

_____

_____

_____

_____

_____

_____

*Today was a wonderful day. Tomorrow
will be even better.*

Something that made me happy today was:

_____

_____

_____

_____

_____

I am capable. I am strong. I am powerful. I am brave.

I know I am:

_____

_____

_____

_____

Date: ___ /___ /_____

Gratitude brings wonderful things into my life.

Today, I am grateful for:

_____

_____

_____

_____

I have the power to choose my thoughts and create my life.

Today, I will focus on:

_____

_____

_____

_____

_____

The Universe is on my side and is always working on my behalf.

I know the Universe is helping me to:

_____

_____

_____

_____

_____

If I can see it and believe in it, I know I can achieve it.

I am in the process of:

_____

_____

_____

_____

_____

_____

I will end each day with positive thoughts and excitement for all that is to come.

Something that made me happy today was:

_____

_____

_____

_____

I am loved. I am valued. I am worthy.

I know I am:

_____

_____

_____

_____

Date: ___ /___ /____

I am so thankful for the way my life is unfolding.

Today, I am grateful for:

_____

_____

_____

_____

I know my thoughts become my life.

Today, I will focus on:

_____

_____

_____

_____

_____

The Universe loves me and wants to bring me all I desire.

I know the Universe is helping me to:

_____

_____

_____

_____

_____

There is nothing I cannot do, have, or be.

I am in the process of:

_____

_____

_____

_____

_____

_____

Each new day is an opportunity to make something wonderful happen.

Something that made me happy today was:

_____

_____

_____

_____

_____

I am surrounded by people who love me and choose me.

I know I am:

_____

_____

_____

_____

Date: ___ /___ /____

I welcome peace, love, and joy into my life.

Today, I am grateful for:

_____

_____

_____

_____

I know positive thoughts turn into positive outcomes.

Today, I will focus on:

_____

_____

_____

_____

_____

I trust the process. Everything comes to me in perfect timing.

I know the Universe is helping me to:

_____

_____

_____

_____

_____

I know success is inevitable. New doors open for me every day.

I am in the process of:

_____

_____

_____

_____

_____

_____

I am grateful for where I am and excited for where I am going.

Something that made me happy today was:

_____

_____

_____

_____

I am everything I need to be. Always.

I know I am:

_____

_____

_____

_____

Date: ___ /___ /_____

I am at peace and in harmony with all I am and all I have.

Today, I am grateful for:

_____

_____

_____

_____

I let go of doubt and fear and celebrate all that is going my way.

Today, I will focus on:

_____

_____

_____

_____

_____

I am loved and worthy of having all I desire.

I know the Universe is helping me to:

_____

_____

_____

_____

_____

I know there are no limits to all I can be and achieve.

I am in the process of:

_____

_____

_____

_____

_____

_____

Today was a wonderful day. Tomorrow
will be even better.

Something that made me happy today was:

_____

_____

_____

_____

_____

I am capable. I am strong. I am powerful. I am brave.

I know I am:

_____

_____

_____

_____

Date: ___ / ___ / _____

Gratitude brings wonderful things into my life.

Today, I am grateful for:

_____

_____

_____

_____

I have the power to choose my thoughts and create my life.

Today, I will focus on:

_____

_____

_____

_____

_____

The Universe is on my side and is always working on my behalf.

I know the Universe is helping me to:

_____

_____

_____

_____

_____

If I can see it and believe in it, I know I can achieve it.

I am in the process of:

_____

_____

_____

_____

_____

_____

I will end each day with positive thoughts and excitement for all that is to come.

Something that made me happy today was:

_____

_____

_____

_____

I am loved. I am valued. I am worthy.

I know I am:

_____

_____

_____

_____

Date: ___ /___ /____

I am so thankful for the way my life is unfolding.

Today, I am grateful for:

_____

_____

_____

_____

I know my thoughts become my life.

Today, I will focus on:

_____

_____

_____

_____

_____

The Universe loves me and wants to bring me all I desire.

I know the Universe is helping me to:

_____

_____

_____

_____

_____

There is nothing I cannot do, have, or be.

I am in the process of:

_____

_____

_____

_____

_____

_____

*Each new day is an opportunity to make something
wonderful happen.*

Something that made me happy today was:

_____

_____

_____

_____

_____

I am surrounded by people who love me and choose me.

I know I am:

_____

_____

_____

_____

Date: ___ /___ /_____

I welcome peace, love, and joy into my life.

Today, I am grateful for:

_____

_____

_____

_____

I know positive thoughts turn into positive outcomes.

Today, I will focus on:

_____

_____

_____

_____

_____

I trust the process. Everything comes to me in perfect timing.

I know the Universe is helping me to:

_____

_____

_____

_____

_____

I know success is inevitable. New doors open for me every day.

I am in the process of:

_____

_____

_____

_____

_____

I am grateful for where I am and excited for where I am going.

Something that made me happy today was:

_____

_____

_____

_____

I am everything I need to be. Always.

I know I am:

_____

_____

_____

_____

Date: ___ /___ /____

I am at peace and in harmony with all I am and all I have.

Today, I am grateful for:

_____

_____

_____

_____

I let go of doubt and fear and celebrate all that is going my way.

Today, I will focus on:

_____

_____

_____

_____

_____

I am loved and worthy of having all I desire.

I know the Universe is helping me to:

_____

_____

_____

_____

_____

I know there are no limits to all I can be and achieve.

I am in the process of:

_____

_____

_____

_____

_____

_____

Today was a wonderful day. Tomorrow
will be even better.

Something that made me happy today was:

_____

_____

_____

_____

_____

I am capable. I am strong. I am powerful. I am brave.

I know I am:

_____

_____

_____

_____

Date: ___ / ___ / _____

Gratitude brings wonderful things into my life.

Today, I am grateful for:

_____

_____

_____

_____

I have the power to choose my thoughts and create my life.

Today, I will focus on:

_____

_____

_____

_____

_____

The Universe is on my side and is always working on my behalf.

I know the Universe is helping me to:

_____

_____

_____

_____

_____

If I can see it and believe in it, I know I can achieve it.

I am in the process of:

_____

_____

_____

_____

_____

_____

*I will end each day with positive thoughts and excitement for
all that is to come.*

Something that made me happy today was:

_____

_____

_____

_____

_____

I am loved. I am valued. I am worthy.

I know I am:

_____

_____

_____

_____

Date: ___ /___ /____

I am so thankful for the way my life is unfolding.

Today, I am grateful for:

_____

_____

_____

_____

I know my thoughts become my life.

Today, I will focus on:

_____

_____

_____

_____

_____

The Universe loves me and wants to bring me all I desire.

I know the Universe is helping me to:

_____

_____

_____

_____

_____

There is nothing I cannot do, have, or be.

I am in the process of:

_____

_____

_____

_____

_____

_____

Each new day is an opportunity to make something wonderful happen.

Something that made me happy today was:

_____

_____

_____

_____

_____

I am surrounded by people who love me and choose me.

I know I am:

_____

_____

_____

_____

Date: ___ /___ /____

I welcome peace, love, and joy into my life.

Today, I am grateful for:

_____

_____

_____

_____

I know positive thoughts turn into positive outcomes.

Today, I will focus on:

_____

_____

_____

_____

_____

I trust the process. Everything comes to me in perfect timing.

I know the Universe is helping me to:

_____

_____

_____

_____

_____

I know success is inevitable. New doors open for me every day.

I am in the process of:

_____

_____

_____

_____

_____

_____

I am grateful for where I am and excited for where I am going.

Something that made me happy today was:

_____

_____

_____

_____

_____

I am everything I need to be. Always.

I know I am:

_____

_____

_____

_____

Date: ____ /____ /_____

I am at peace and in harmony with all I am and all I have.

Today, I am grateful for:

_____

_____

_____

_____

I let go of doubt and fear and celebrate all that is going my way.

Today, I will focus on:

_____

_____

_____

_____

_____

I am loved and worthy of having all I desire.

I know the Universe is helping me to:

_____

_____

_____

_____

_____

I know there are no limits to all I can be and achieve.

I am in the process of:

_____

_____

_____

_____

_____

_____

*Today was a wonderful day. Tomorrow
will be even better.*

Something that made me happy today was:

_____

_____

_____

_____

_____

I am capable. I am strong. I am powerful. I am brave.

I know I am:

_____

_____

_____

_____

Date: ___ /___ /_____

Gratitude brings wonderful things into my life.

Today, I am grateful for:

_____

_____

_____

_____

I have the power to choose my thoughts and create my life.

Today, I will focus on:

_____

_____

_____

_____

_____

The Universe is on my side and is always working on my behalf.

I know the Universe is helping me to:

_____

_____

_____

_____

_____

If I can see it and believe in it, I know I can achieve it.

I am in the process of:

_____

_____

_____

_____

_____

_____

I will end each day with positive thoughts and excitement for all that is to come.

Something that made me happy today was:

_____

_____

_____

_____

I am loved. I am valued. I am worthy.

I know I am:

_____

_____

_____

_____

Date: ___ / ___ / ____

I am so thankful for the way my life is unfolding.

Today, I am grateful for:

_____

_____

_____

_____

I know my thoughts become my life.

Today, I will focus on:

_____

_____

_____

_____

_____

The Universe loves me and wants to bring me all I desire.

I know the Universe is helping me to:

_____

_____

_____

_____

There is nothing I cannot do, have, or be.

I am in the process of:

_____

_____

_____

_____

_____

_____

Each new day is an opportunity to make something wonderful happen.

Something that made me happy today was:

_____

_____

_____

_____

_____

I am surrounded by people who love me and choose me.

I know I am:

_____

_____

_____

_____

Date: ___ /___ /____

I welcome peace, love, and joy into my life.

Today, I am grateful for:

_____

_____

_____

_____

I know positive thoughts turn into positive outcomes.

Today, I will focus on:

_____

_____

_____

_____

_____

I trust the process. Everything comes to me in perfect timing.

I know the Universe is helping me to:

_____

_____

_____

_____

_____

I know success is inevitable. New doors open for me every day.

I am in the process of:

_____

_____

_____

_____

_____

_____

I am grateful for where I am and excited for where I am going.

Something that made me happy today was:

_____

_____

_____

_____

I am everything I need to be. Always.

I know I am:

_____

_____

_____

_____

Date: ___ /___ /____

I am at peace and in harmony with all I am and all I have.

Today, I am grateful for:

_____

_____

_____

_____

I let go of doubt and fear and celebrate all that is going my way.

Today, I will focus on:

_____

_____

_____

_____

_____

I am loved and worthy of having all I desire.

I know the Universe is helping me to:

_____

_____

_____

_____

_____

I know there are no limits to all I can be and achieve.

I am in the process of:

_____

_____

_____

_____

_____

_____

*Today was a wonderful day. Tomorrow
will be even better.*

Something that made me happy today was:

_____

_____

_____

_____

_____

I am capable. I am strong. I am powerful. I am brave.

I know I am:

_____

_____

_____

_____

Date: ___ / ___ / ____

Gratitude brings wonderful things into my life.

Today, I am grateful for:

_____

_____

_____

_____

I have the power to choose my thoughts and create my life.

Today, I will focus on:

_____

_____

_____

_____

_____

The Universe is on my side and is always working on my behalf.

I know the Universe is helping me to:

_____

_____

_____

_____

_____

If I can see it and believe in it, I know I can achieve it.

I am in the process of:

_____

_____

_____

_____

_____

_____

I will end each day with positive thoughts and excitement for all that is to come.

Something that made me happy today was:

_____

_____

_____

_____

_____

I am loved. I am valued. I am worthy.

I know I am:

_____

_____

_____

_____

Date: ___ /___ /____

I am so thankful for the way my life is unfolding.

Today, I am grateful for:

_____

_____

_____

I know my thoughts become my life.

Today, I will focus on:

_____

_____

_____

_____

The Universe loves me and wants to bring me all I desire.

I know the Universe is helping me to:

_____

_____

_____

_____

There is nothing I cannot do, have, or be.

I am in the process of:

_____

_____

_____

_____

_____

_____

Each new day is an opportunity to make something wonderful happen.

Something that made me happy today was:

_____

_____

_____

_____

_____

I am surrounded by people who love me and choose me.

I know I am:

_____

_____

_____

_____

Date: ___ /___ /____

I welcome peace, love, and joy into my life.

Today, I am grateful for:

_____

_____

_____

_____

I know positive thoughts turn into positive outcomes.

Today, I will focus on:

_____

_____

_____

_____

_____

I trust the process. Everything comes to me in perfect timing.

I know the Universe is helping me to:

_____

_____

_____

_____

_____

I know success is inevitable. New doors open for me every day.

I am in the process of:

_____

_____

_____

_____

_____

_____

I am grateful for where I am and excited for
where I am going.

Something that made me happy today was:

_____

_____

_____

_____

I am everything I need to be. Always.

I know I am:

_____

_____

_____

_____

Date: ____ /____ /_____

I am at peace and in harmony with all I am and all I have.

Today, I am grateful for:

_____

_____

_____

_____

I let go of doubt and fear and celebrate all that is going my way.

Today, I will focus on:

_____

_____

_____

_____

_____

I am loved and worthy of having all I desire.

I know the Universe is helping me to:

_____

_____

_____

_____

_____

I know there are no limits to all I can be and achieve.

I am in the process of:

_____

_____

_____

_____

_____

Today was a wonderful day. Tomorrow
will be even better.

Something that made me happy today was:

_____

_____

_____

_____

I am capable. I am strong. I am powerful. I am brave.

I know I am:

_____

_____

_____

_____

Date: ____ / ____ / _____

Gratitude brings wonderful things into my life.

Today, I am grateful for:

_____

_____

_____

_____

I have the power to choose my thoughts and create my life.

Today, I will focus on:

_____

_____

_____

_____

_____

The Universe is on my side and is always working on my behalf.

I know the Universe is helping me to:

_____

_____

_____

_____

_____

If I can see it and believe in it, I know I can achieve it.

I am in the process of:

_____

_____

_____

_____

_____

_____

I will end each day with positive thoughts and excitement for all that is to come.

Something that made me happy today was:

_____

_____

_____

_____

I am loved. I am valued. I am worthy.

I know I am:

_____

_____

_____

_____

Date: ___ / ___ / ____

I am so thankful for the way my life is unfolding.

Today, I am grateful for:

_____

_____

_____

_____

I know my thoughts become my life.

Today, I will focus on:

_____

_____

_____

_____

_____

The Universe loves me and wants to bring me all I desire.

I know the Universe is helping me to:

_____

_____

_____

_____

_____

There is nothing I cannot do, have, or be.

I am in the process of:

_____

_____

_____

_____

_____

_____

Each new day is an opportunity to make something wonderful happen.

Something that made me happy today was:

_____

_____

_____

_____

_____

I am surrounded by people who love me and choose me.

I know I am:

_____

_____

_____

_____

Date: ___ /___ /____

I welcome peace, love, and joy into my life.

Today, I am grateful for:

_____

_____

_____

_____

I know positive thoughts turn into positive outcomes.

Today, I will focus on:

_____

_____

_____

_____

_____

I trust the process. Everything comes to me in perfect timing.

I know the Universe is helping me to:

_____

_____

_____

_____

_____

I know success is inevitable. New doors open for me every day.

I am in the process of:

_____

_____

_____

_____

_____

_____

I am grateful for where I am and excited for where I am going.

Something that made me happy today was:

_____

_____

_____

_____

I am everything I need to be. Always.

I know I am:

_____

_____

_____

_____

Date: ___ / ___ / _____

I am at peace and in harmony with all I am and all I have.

Today, I am grateful for:

_____

_____

_____

_____

I let go of doubt and fear and celebrate all that is going my way.

Today, I will focus on:

_____

_____

_____

_____

_____

I am loved and worthy of having all I desire.

I know the Universe is helping me to:

_____

_____

_____

_____

_____

I know there are no limits to all I can be and achieve.

I am in the process of:

_____

_____

_____

_____

_____

_____

Today was a wonderful day. Tomorrow
will be even better.

Something that made me happy today was:

_____

_____

_____

_____

_____

I am capable. I am strong. I am powerful. I am brave.

I know I am:

_____

_____

_____

_____

Date: ___ /___ /____

Gratitude brings wonderful things into my life.

Today, I am grateful for:

_____

_____

_____

_____

I have the power to choose my thoughts and create my life.

Today, I will focus on:

_____

_____

_____

_____

_____

The Universe is on my side and is always working on my behalf.

I know the Universe is helping me to:

_____

_____

_____

_____

_____

If I can see it and believe in it, I know I can achieve it.

I am in the process of:

_____

_____

_____

_____

_____

_____

I will end each day with positive thoughts and excitement for all that is to come.

Something that made me happy today was:

_____

_____

_____

_____

I am loved. I am valued. I am worthy.

I know I am:

_____

_____

_____

Date: ___ /___ /____

I am so thankful for the way my life is unfolding.

Today, I am grateful for:

_____

_____

_____

_____

I know my thoughts become my life.

Today, I will focus on:

_____

_____

_____

_____

_____

The Universe loves me and wants to bring me all I desire.

I know the Universe is helping me to:

_____

_____

_____

_____

_____

There is nothing I cannot do, have, or be.

I am in the process of:

_____

_____

_____

_____

_____

_____

Each new day is an opportunity to make something wonderful happen.

Something that made me happy today was:

_____

_____

_____

_____

_____

I am surrounded by people who love me and choose me.

I know I am:

_____

_____

_____

_____

Date: ___ /___ /____

I welcome peace, love, and joy into my life.

Today, I am grateful for:

_____

_____

_____

_____

I know positive thoughts turn into positive outcomes.

Today, I will focus on:

_____

_____

_____

_____

_____

I trust the process. Everything comes to me in perfect timing.

I know the Universe is helping me to:

_____

_____

_____

_____

_____

I know success is inevitable. New doors open for me every day.

I am in the process of:

_____

_____

_____

_____

_____

_____

*I am grateful for where I am and excited for
where I am going.*

Something that made me happy today was:

_____

_____

_____

_____

_____

I am everything I need to be. Always.

I know I am:

_____

_____

_____

_____

Date: ___ /___ /____

I am at peace and in harmony with all I am and all I have.

Today, I am grateful for:

_____

_____

_____

_____

I let go of doubt and fear and celebrate all that is going my way.

Today, I will focus on:

_____

_____

_____

_____

_____

I am loved and worthy of having all I desire.

I know the Universe is helping me to:

_____

_____

_____

_____

_____

I know there are no limits to all I can be and achieve.

I am in the process of:

_____

_____

_____

_____

_____

_____

Today was a wonderful day. Tomorrow will be even better.

Something that made me happy today was:

_____

_____

_____

_____

_____

I am capable. I am strong. I am powerful. I am brave.

I know I am:

_____

_____

_____

_____

Date: ____ / ____ / _____

Gratitude brings wonderful things into my life.

Today, I am grateful for:

_____

_____

_____

_____

I have the power to choose my thoughts and create my life.

Today, I will focus on:

_____

_____

_____

_____

_____

The Universe is on my side and is always working on my behalf.

I know the Universe is helping me to:

_____

_____

_____

_____

_____

If I can see it and believe in it, I know I can achieve it.

I am in the process of:

_____

_____

_____

_____

_____

_____

I will end each day with positive thoughts and excitement for all that is to come.

Something that made me happy today was:

_____

_____

_____

_____

_____

I am loved. I am valued. I am worthy.

I know I am:

_____

_____

_____

_____

Date: ___ /___ /____

I am so thankful for the way my life is unfolding.

Today, I am grateful for:

_____

_____

_____

_____

I know my thoughts become my life.

Today, I will focus on:

_____

_____

_____

_____

_____

The Universe loves me and wants to bring me all I desire.

I know the Universe is helping me to:

_____

_____

_____

_____

_____

There is nothing I cannot do, have, or be.

I am in the process of:

_____

_____

_____

_____

_____

_____

Each new day is an opportunity to make something wonderful happen.

Something that made me happy today was:

_____

_____

_____

_____

_____

I am surrounded by people who love me and choose me.

I know I am:

_____

_____

_____

_____

Date: ___ /___ /____

I welcome peace, love, and joy into my life.

Today, I am grateful for:

_____
_____
_____
_____

I know positive thoughts turn into positive outcomes.

Today, I will focus on:

_____
_____
_____
_____
_____

I trust the process. Everything comes to me in perfect timing.

I know the Universe is helping me to:

_____
_____
_____
_____
_____

I know success is inevitable. New doors open for me every day.

I am in the process of:

_____

_____

_____

_____

_____

_____

I am grateful for where I am and excited for where I am going.

Something that made me happy today was:

_____

_____

_____

_____

_____

I am everything I need to be. Always.

I know I am:

_____

_____

_____

_____

Date: ___ /___ /____

I am at peace and in harmony with all I am and all I have.

Today, I am grateful for:

_____

_____

_____

_____

I let go of doubt and fear and celebrate all that is going my way.

Today, I will focus on:

_____

_____

_____

_____

_____

I am loved and worthy of having all I desire.

I know the Universe is helping me to:

_____

_____

_____

_____

_____

I know there are no limits to all I can be and achieve.

I am in the process of:

_____

_____

_____

_____

_____

_____

*Today was a wonderful day. Tomorrow
will be even better.*

Something that made me happy today was:

_____

_____

_____

_____

I am capable. I am strong. I am powerful. I am brave.

I know I am:

_____

_____

_____

_____

Date: ___ / ___ / _____

Gratitude brings wonderful things into my life.

Today, I am grateful for:

_____

_____

_____

_____

I have the power to choose my thoughts and create my life.

Today, I will focus on:

_____

_____

_____

_____

_____

The Universe is on my side and is always working on my behalf.

I know the Universe is helping me to:

_____

_____

_____

_____

_____

If I can see it and believe in it, I know I can achieve it.

I am in the process of:

_____

_____

_____

_____

_____

_____

I will end each day with positive thoughts and excitement for all that is to come.

Something that made me happy today was:

_____

_____

_____

_____

_____

I am loved. I am valued. I am worthy.

I know I am:

_____

_____

_____

_____

Date: ___ /___ /____

I am so thankful for the way my life is unfolding.

Today, I am grateful for:

_____

_____

_____

_____

I know my thoughts become my life.

Today, I will focus on:

_____

_____

_____

_____

_____

The Universe loves me and wants to bring me all I desire.

I know the Universe is helping me to:

_____

_____

_____

_____

_____

There is nothing I cannot do, have, or be.

I am in the process of:

_____

_____

_____

_____

_____

_____

Each new day is an opportunity to make something wonderful happen.

Something that made me happy today was:

_____

_____

_____

_____

_____

I am surrounded by people who love me and choose me.

I know I am:

_____

_____

_____

_____

Date: ___ / ___ / ____

I welcome peace, love, and joy into my life.

Today, I am grateful for:

_____

_____

_____

_____

I know positive thoughts turn into positive outcomes.

Today, I will focus on:

_____

_____

_____

_____

_____

I trust the process. Everything comes to me in perfect timing.

I know the Universe is helping me to:

_____

_____

_____

_____

_____

I know success is inevitable. New doors open for me every day.

I am in the process of:

_____

_____

_____

_____

_____

_____

*I am grateful for where I am and excited for
where I am going.*

Something that made me happy today was:

_____

_____

_____

_____

_____

I am everything I need to be. Always.

I know I am:

_____

_____

_____

_____

Date: ___ /___ /____

I am at peace and in harmony with all I am and all I have.

Today, I am grateful for:

_____

_____

_____

_____

I let go of doubt and fear and celebrate all that is going my way.

Today, I will focus on:

_____

_____

_____

_____

_____

I am loved and worthy of having all I desire.

I know the Universe is helping me to:

_____

_____

_____

_____

_____

I know there are no limits to all I can be and achieve.

I am in the process of:

_____

_____

_____

_____

_____

_____

*Today was a wonderful day. Tomorrow
will be even better.*

Something that made me happy today was:

_____

_____

_____

_____

_____

I am capable. I am strong. I am powerful. I am brave.

I know I am:

_____

_____

_____

_____

Date: ___ / ___ / ____

Gratitude brings wonderful things into my life.

Today, I am grateful for:

_____

_____

_____

_____

I have the power to choose my thoughts and create my life.

Today, I will focus on:

_____

_____

_____

_____

_____

The Universe is on my side and is always working on my behalf.

I know the Universe is helping me to:

_____

_____

_____

_____

_____

If I can see it and believe in it, I know I can achieve it.

I am in the process of:

_____

_____

_____

_____

_____

_____

I will end each day with positive thoughts and excitement for all that is to come.

Something that made me happy today was:

_____

_____

_____

_____

I am loved. I am valued. I am worthy.

I know I am:

_____

_____

_____

_____

Date: ___ /___ /____

I am so thankful for the way my life is unfolding.

Today, I am grateful for:

_____

_____

_____

_____

I know my thoughts become my life.

Today, I will focus on:

_____

_____

_____

_____

_____

The Universe loves me and wants to bring me all I desire.

I know the Universe is helping me to:

_____

_____

_____

_____

_____

There is nothing I cannot do, have, or be.

I am in the process of:

_____

_____

_____

_____

_____

_____

*Each new day is an opportunity to make something
wonderful happen.*

Something that made me happy today was:

_____

_____

_____

_____

_____

I am surrounded by people who love me and choose me.

I know I am:

_____

_____

_____

_____

Date: ___ /___ /____

I welcome peace, love, and joy into my life.

Today, I am grateful for:

_____

_____

_____

_____

I know positive thoughts turn into positive outcomes.

Today, I will focus on:

_____

_____

_____

_____

_____

I trust the process. Everything comes to me in perfect timing.

I know the Universe is helping me to:

_____

_____

_____

_____

_____

I know success is inevitable. New doors open for me every day.

I am in the process of:

_____

_____

_____

_____

_____

_____

I am grateful for where I am and excited for where I am going.

Something that made me happy today was:

_____

_____

_____

_____

_____

I am everything I need to be. Always.

I know I am:

_____

_____

_____

_____

Date: ___ /___ /____

I am at peace and in harmony with all I am and all I have.

Today, I am grateful for:

_____

_____

_____

_____

I let go of doubt and fear and celebrate all that is going my way.

Today, I will focus on:

_____

_____

_____

_____

_____

I am loved and worthy of having all I desire.

I know the Universe is helping me to:

_____

_____

_____

_____

_____

I know there are no limits to all I can be and achieve.

I am in the process of:

_____

_____

_____

_____

_____

_____

*Today was a wonderful day. Tomorrow
will be even better.*

Something that made me happy today was:

_____

_____

_____

_____

_____

I am capable. I am strong. I am powerful. I am brave.

I know I am:

_____

_____

_____

_____

www.ingramcontent.com/pod-product-compliance
Lightning Source LLC
Chambersburg PA
CBHW051632120626
46551CB00014B/2038